Life in a
GL🌐BAL
VILLAGE

Gary Miller

ISBN: 978-1-941213-30-8
Cover design and layout: Teresa Sommers
Printed in Mexico

Published by:
TGS International
P.O. Box 355
Berlin, Ohio 44610 USA
Phone: 330-893-4828
Fax: 330-893-2305
www.tgsinternational.com

TGS000899

Contents

What Is "Normal," Anyway?

Our neighbors influence our lives. We watch what they do and where they go, and their choices sway us. For instance, when we hear someone talk about a "big house," our mental image of that house depends on what is normal in our culture. A "big house" in the Republic of Congo means something entirely different than a "big house" in America. Our neighbors' lifestyles become reference points for our own.

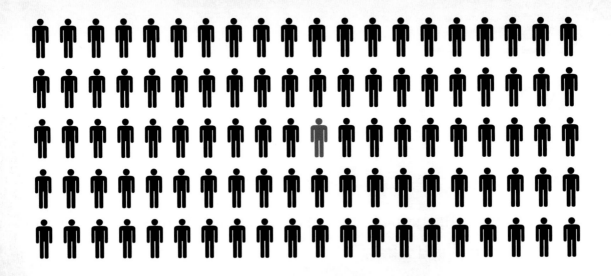

With that in mind, suppose the whole world were shrunk down to a village of just 100 people. How would living in this village affect your daily choices and lifestyle?

IMAGINE THE WORLD SHRUNK TO A VILLAGE OF

100

PEOPLE

What if, when you looked out your bedroom window each morning, your neighbor's house looked something like this?

Or what if you walked out your
front door and saw a neighborhood
that looked like this? How might
this affect your feelings about
the home you live in now?

What if this man were your
neighbor on his way to work?

Or what if you backed your truck out
of the garage and headed off to work,
only to see your neighbor already hard
at work? Would it make you more content
with your present pickup? When you need
to purchase another vehicle, would your
neighbor's situation influence your choice?

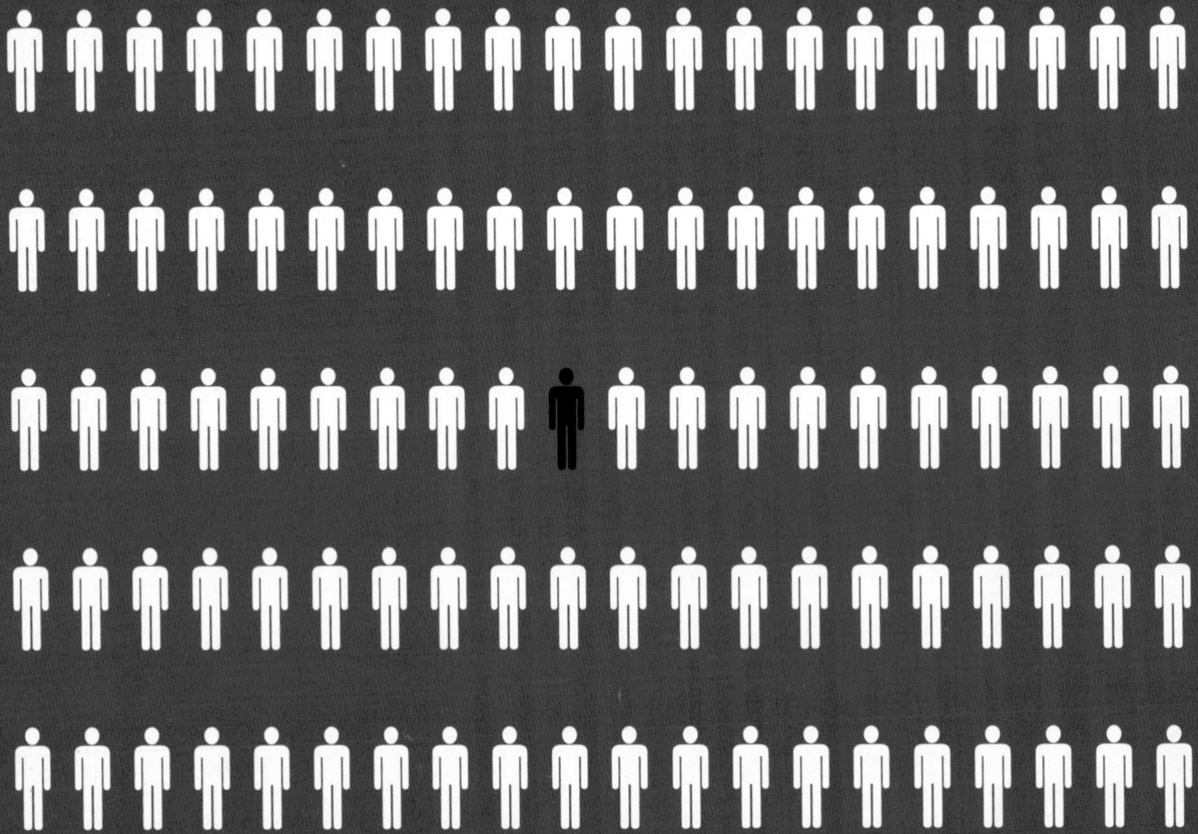

Your Neighbors in the Global Village

Imagine yourself in the middle of this global village of 100 people. Each figure on the diagram represents 70 million people living today.

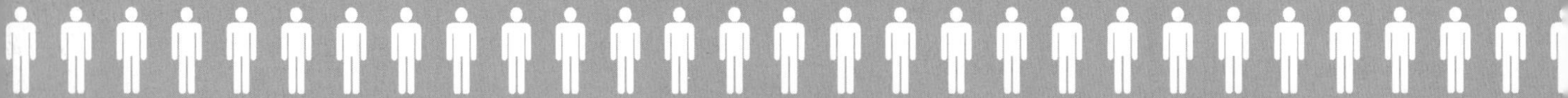

AGE

Let's start by getting a picture
of the age of the people in your
village. [1, 2, 3, 4, 5, 6]

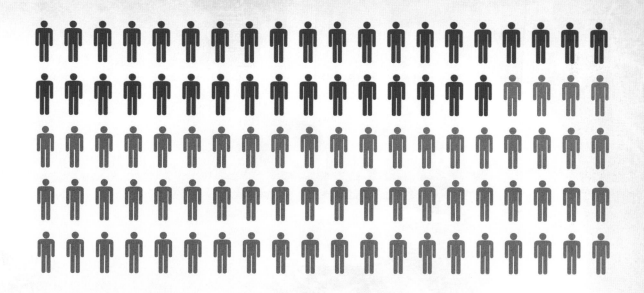

In your village of 100, 10 of the
citizens are less than 5 years old,
and 36 are under 20 years old.

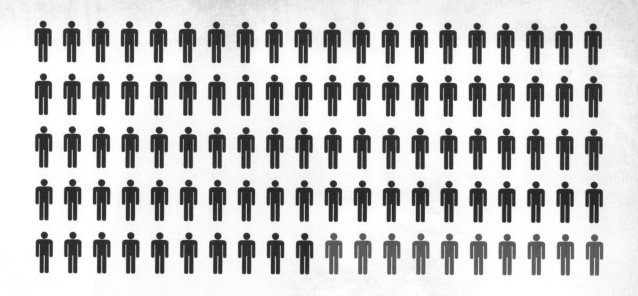

Sixty-nine people are under 40 years old,
and 90 people in the village are under 60.
Only 10 people are over 60 years old.

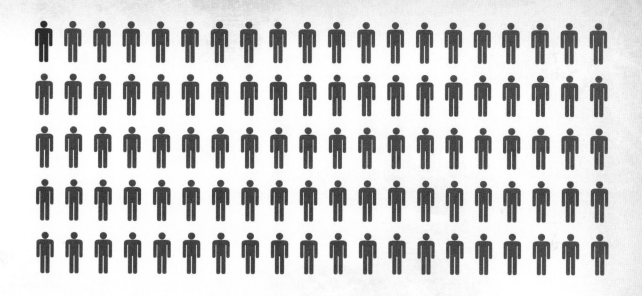

If you are over 80 years old, you
are the only one. In many countries
few people live this long.

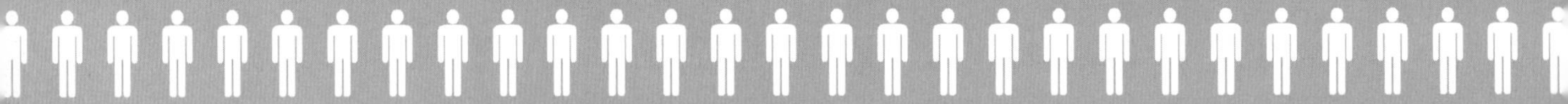

NATIONALITY

What about nationality? What do the
people in your village look like?

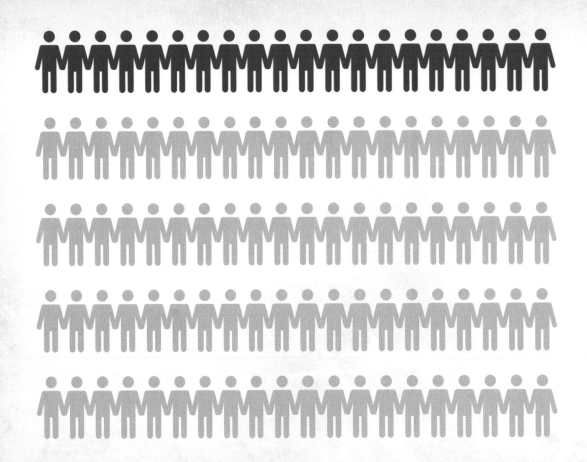

20

Twenty of them are Chinese.

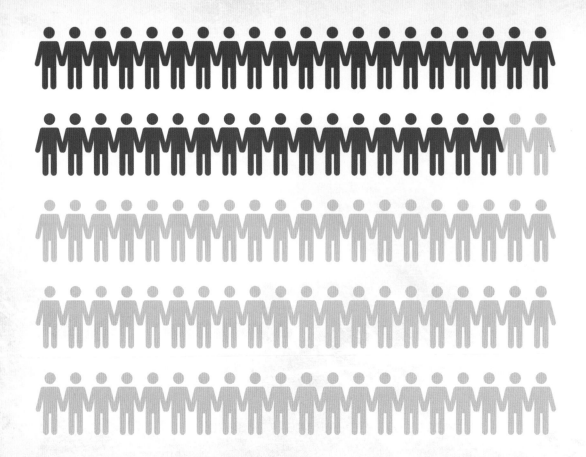

18

Eighteen are from India. Notice that
38 people in your village originate
from just China and India.

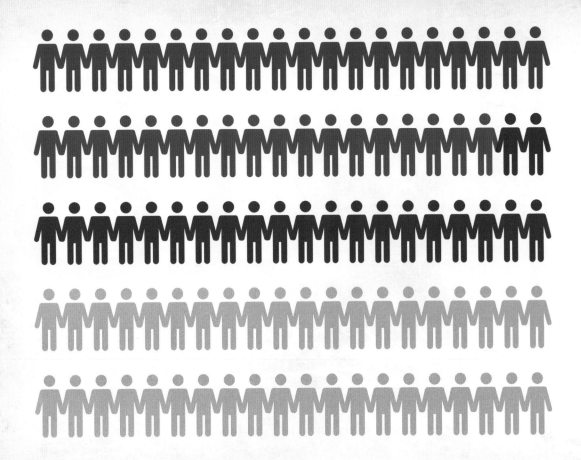

22

Twenty-two are from the rest of Asia,
including countries like Bangladesh,
Myanmar, and Indonesia. This means 60
people in your village come from Asia.

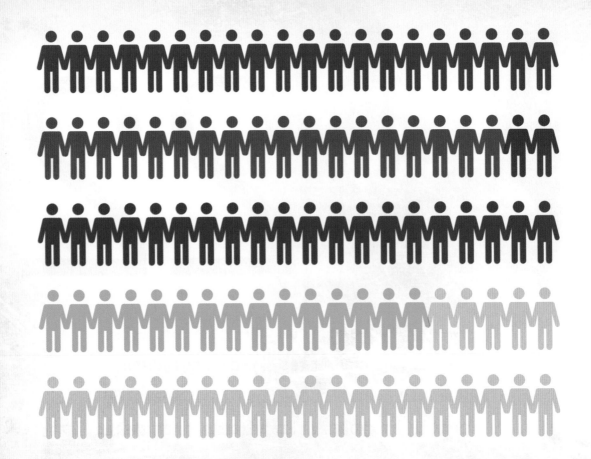

15

Fifteen of your neighbors are from Africa.

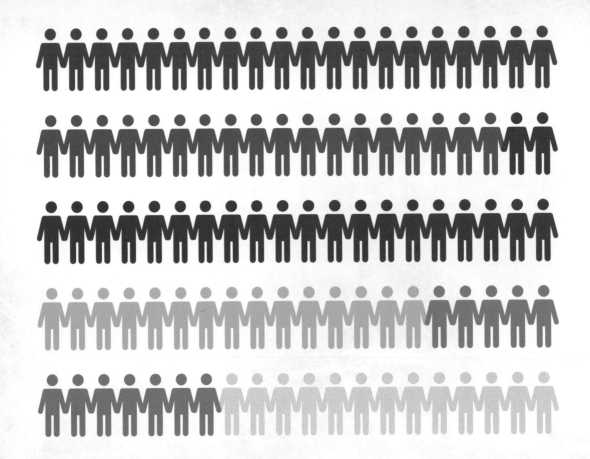

12

Twelve people are from Europe, including Russia.

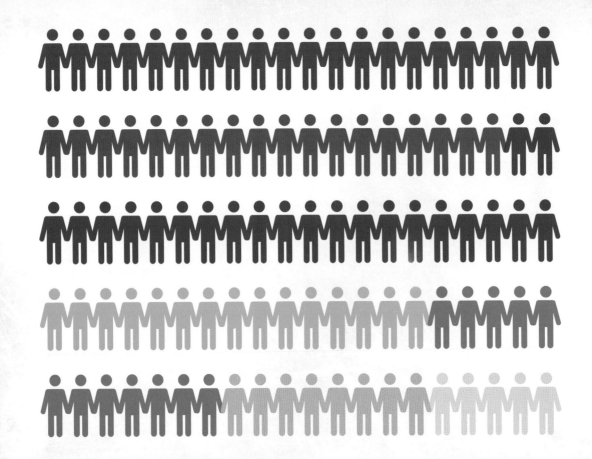

8

Eight people in your village were
born in Central and South America.

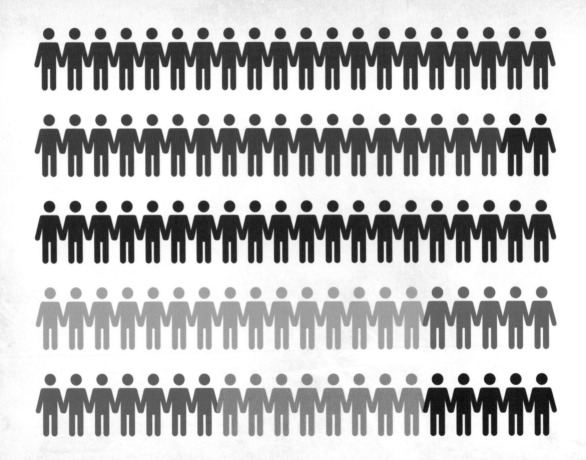

5

Finally, only five people in your village are from North America. We who live in the United States may think we are a big part of the world; in a global village, we are a small minority.

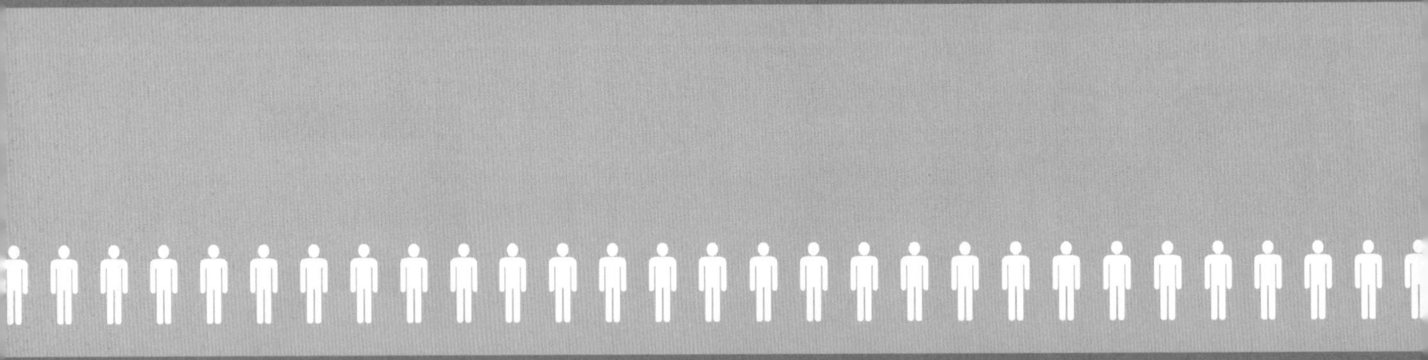

RELIGION

What kind of religious beliefs do
the people in your village have? [7, 8]

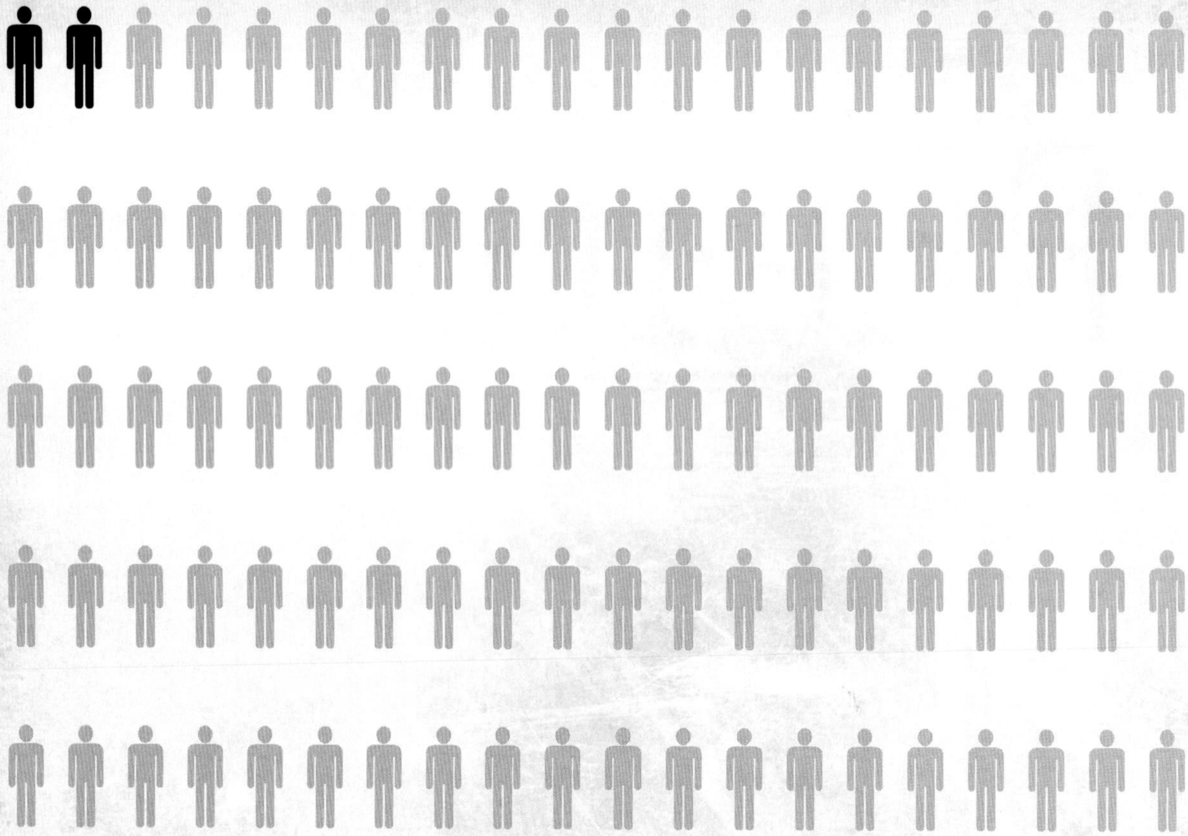

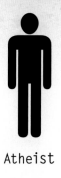

Atheist

Two are atheists, who say there is no God.

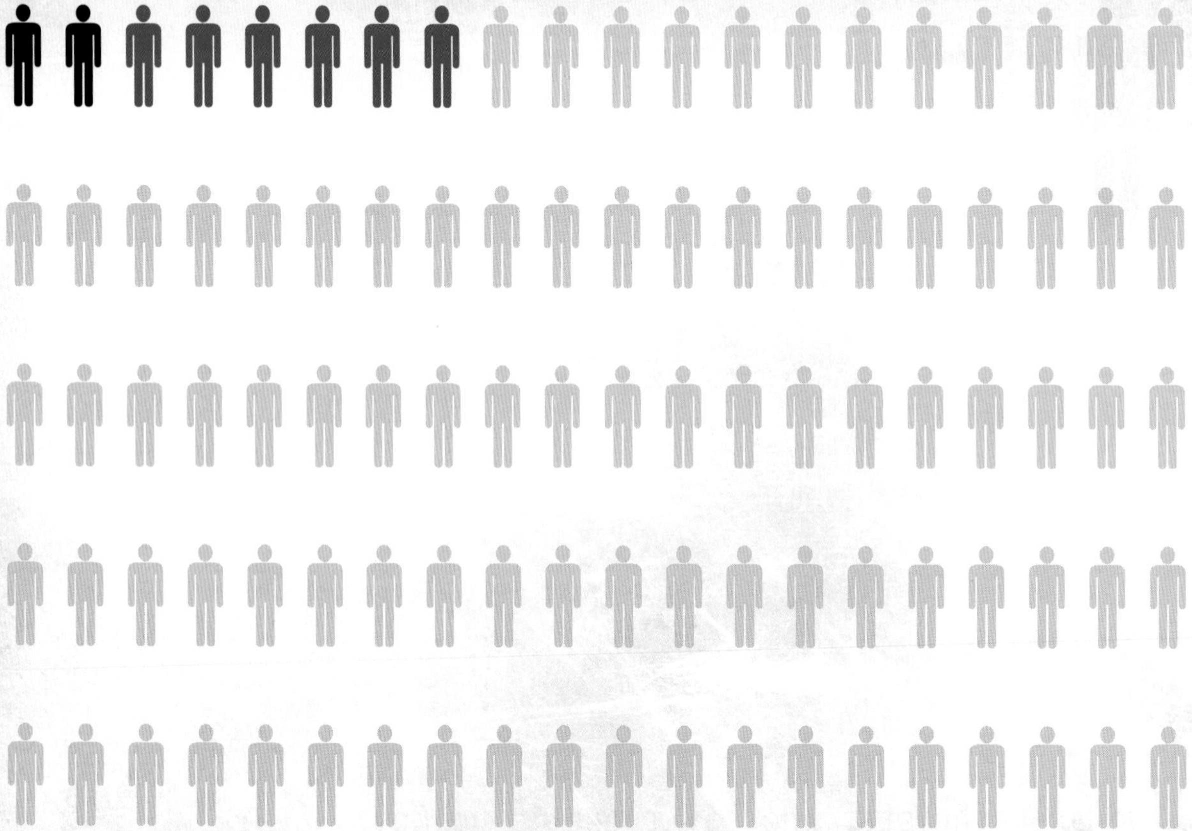

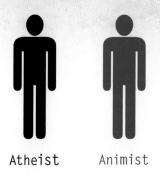

Atheist   Animist

Six people are animists. They believe God exists in animals, plants, and inanimate objects like rocks and trees. This false belief about God is held by more people than the total population of North America.

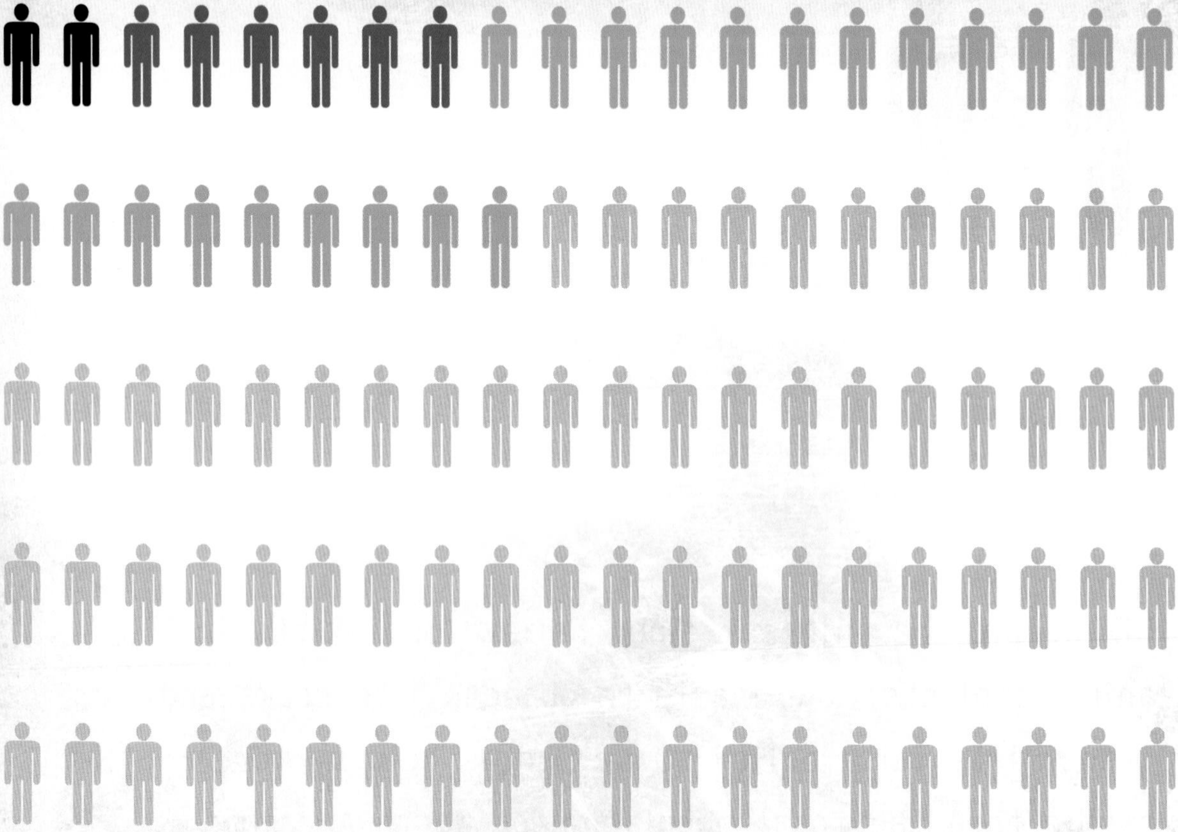

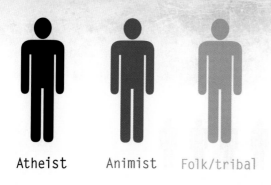

Atheist   Animist   Folk/tribal

Twenty-one people in your village adhere to folk and tribal
religions. Some of these are similar to animism, but their
mix of beliefs falls outside the more orthodox religions.

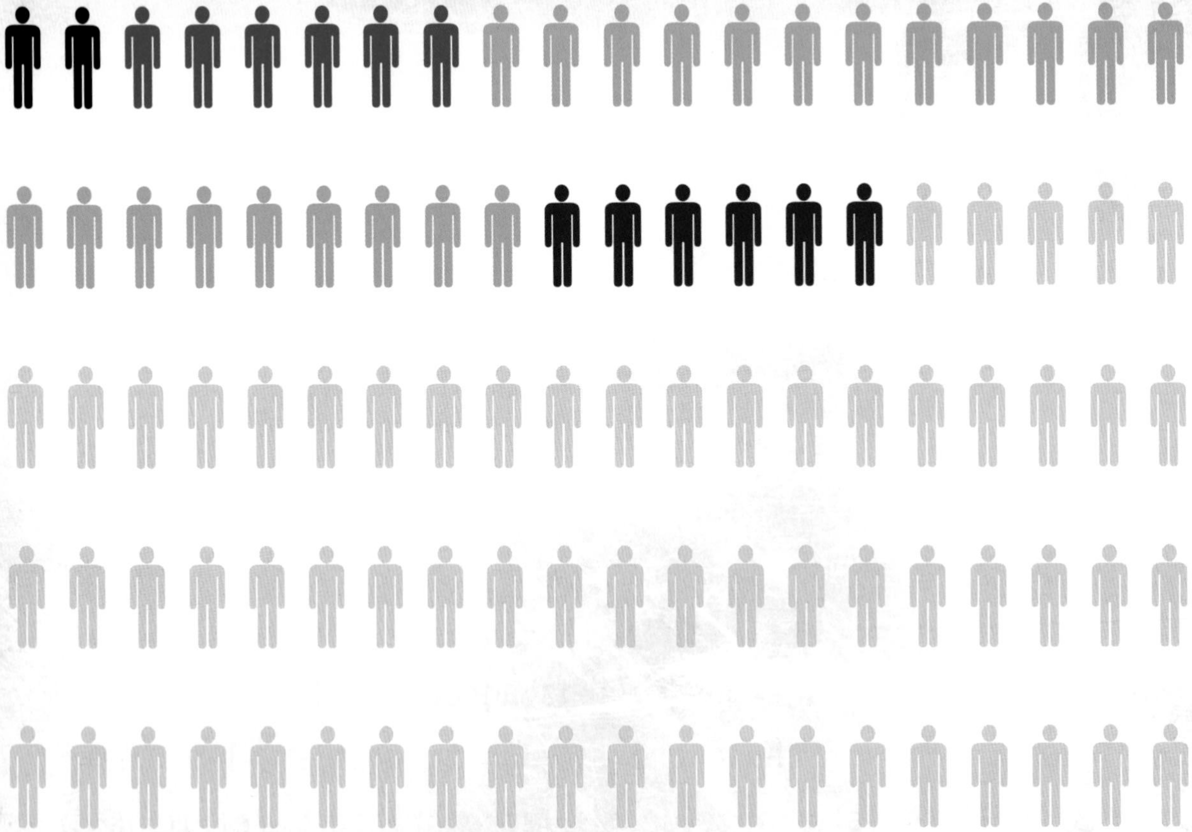

Atheist   Animist   Folk/tribal   Buddhist

Six of your neighbors proclaim themselves Buddhists, or
followers of Gautama Buddha. Buddhists do not worship
one creator god. Rather, they believe beings go through a
succession of lifetimes in different forms, a process known
as reincarnation. Some Buddhists are opposed to harming
anything living—they do not intentionally kill even insects.

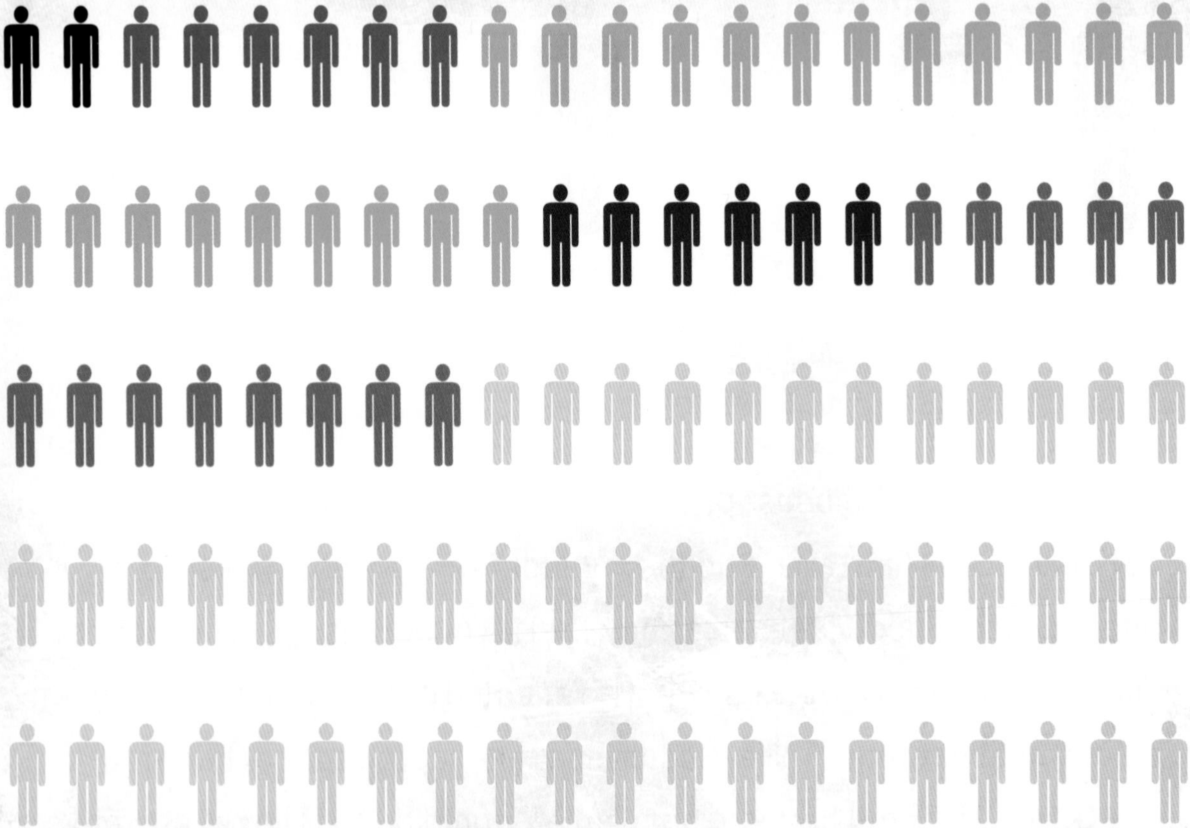

Atheist Animist Folk/tribal Buddhist Hindu

Thirteen of your neighbors are Hindus, and most of them come from India. Hinduism is a unique religion that does not claim a founder, does not worship any one god, and does not follow any one set of religious rites. Some say it is primarily a way of life. These neighbors believe cows are holy and anyone who kills one deserves death.

[54]

Atheist   Animist   Folk/tribal   Buddhist   Hindu   Muslim

Twenty people, or one-fifth of your village, practice the Islamic faith. They are followers of a man named Muhammad, who lived about 600 years after Jesus. Muslims believe in one god, Allah, and study a book called the Koran. They believe this book contains a holy revelation from Allah.

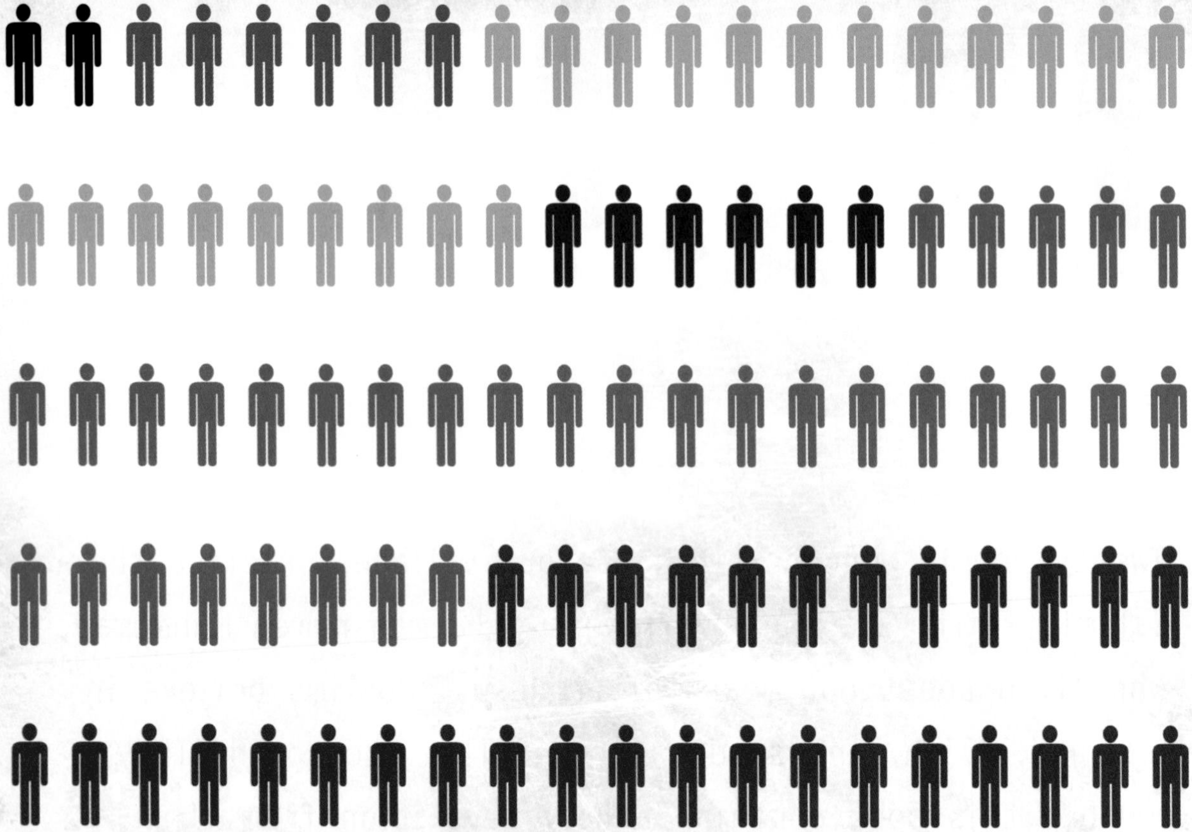

Atheist   Animist   Folk/tribal   Buddhist   Hindu   Muslim   Christian

The remaining 32 people in your village profess belief in Jesus Christ. However, there is a wide variety in how they practice their beliefs. Let's look at the denominational lines which divide this 32% of our world.

WHO ARE THE 32?

51% are Roman Catholic.

26.4% are Protestant.

14% are Orthodox.

4% are Anglican.

4.5% belong to miscellaneous professing groups, including Mormons, Jehovah's Witnesses, and other denominations.

Approximately 0.1% belong to some type of Anabaptist fellowship.

Remember, these figures are not percentages of the total world, but of the 32 who claim to follow Jesus. [9, 10, 11, 12]

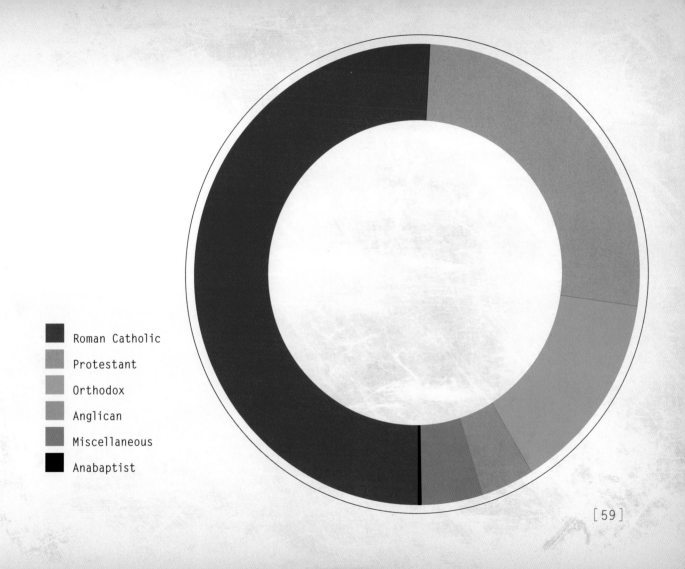

Roman Catholic

Protestant

Orthodox

Anglican

Miscellaneous

Anabaptist

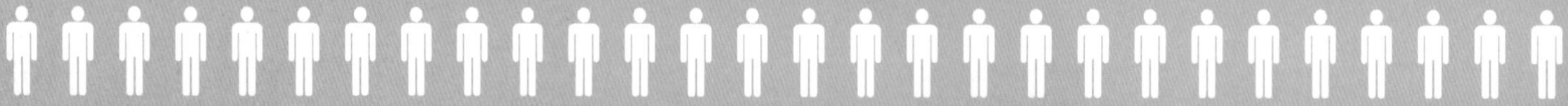

LIFESTYLE

What about living conditions? How does your lifestyle compare to others living in your village?

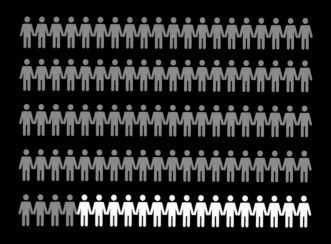

No Access to Clean Drinking Water

While many have to walk long distances for drinking water, 16 people in your village do not have any source of clean drinking water at all.[13] The water they drink and cook with is polluted.

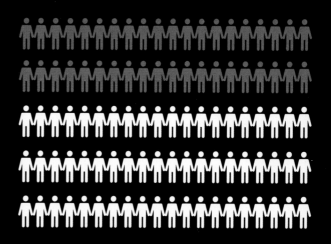

No Access to Toilets

Sixty villagers have no access to a toilet.[14] This does not mean merely that they don't have a toilet in their houses; it means there is none available to them in their entire community.

Do Not Have Toilet Paper

Even more people in your village, 73, do not have toilet paper. Lack of clean water and proper sanitation kills children at an estimated rate equivalent to a jumbo jet crashing every three hours.[15, 16]

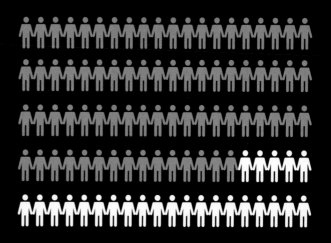

No Access to a Cell Phone

Twenty-five people in your village have no access to a cell phone.[17] That means there are many more cell phones than toilets.

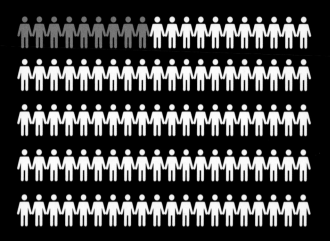

Don't Own a Personal Vehicle

Ninety-one people in your village do not own a personal vehicle.[18, 19] If you are one of the 9 who does, you might be giving your neighbors a lot of rides.

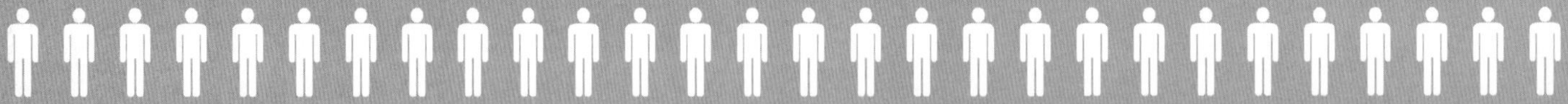

INCOME

What about income in your village?

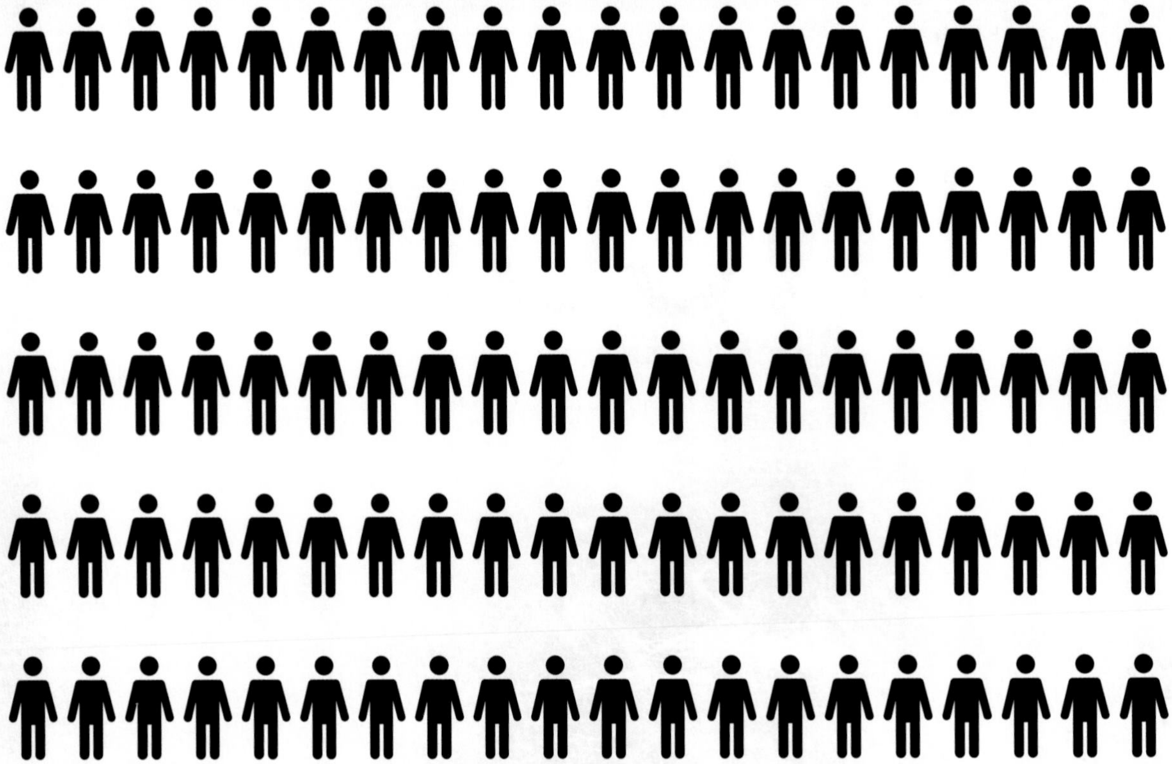

Imagine that the wealthiest people are in the top row and the poorest in the bottom row. Which row do you think you are in?

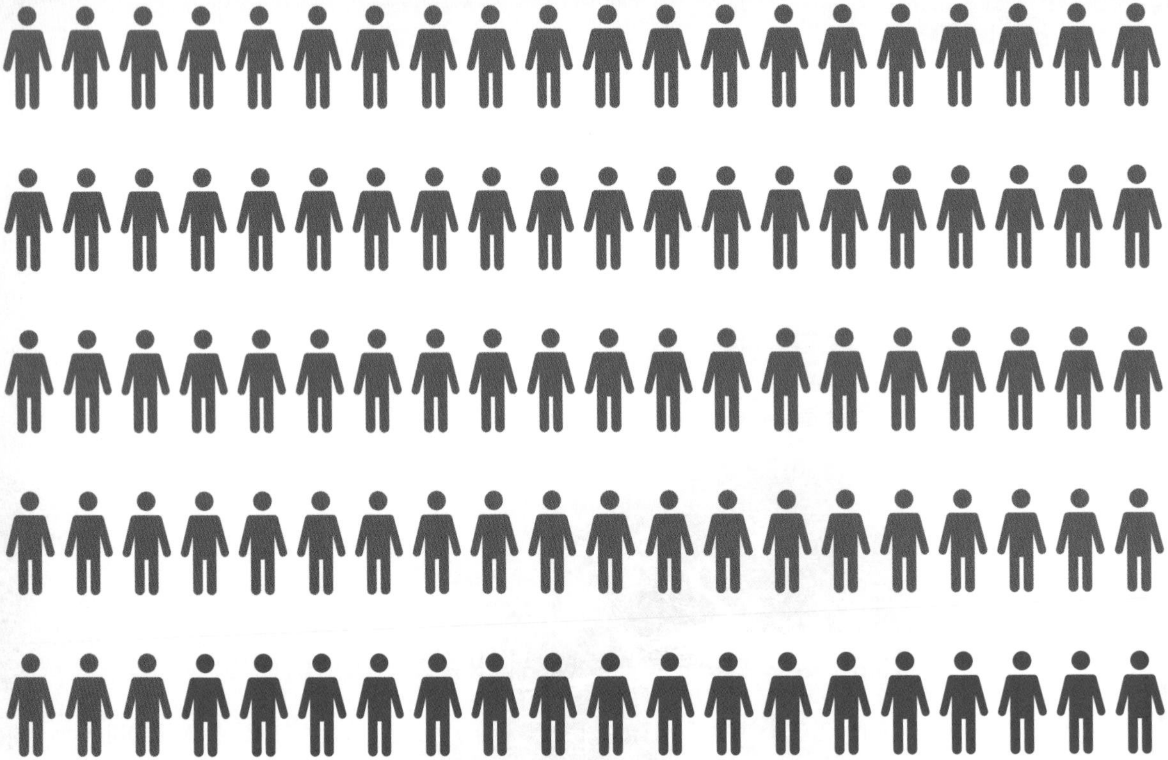

Seventeen people in your village earn less than $1.25 per day—that is, if they can find work.[20, 21] Let's visit one of these neighbors.

This Cambodian woman supports her family by making baskets. She goes out early each morning and harvests the long-stemmed weeds you see on the ground beside her. Using a knife, she removes the outer bark and then weaves the stems into a basket. By working quickly, she can produce one of these baskets each day. The basket sells for about $1 US in the market. This is her only source of income.

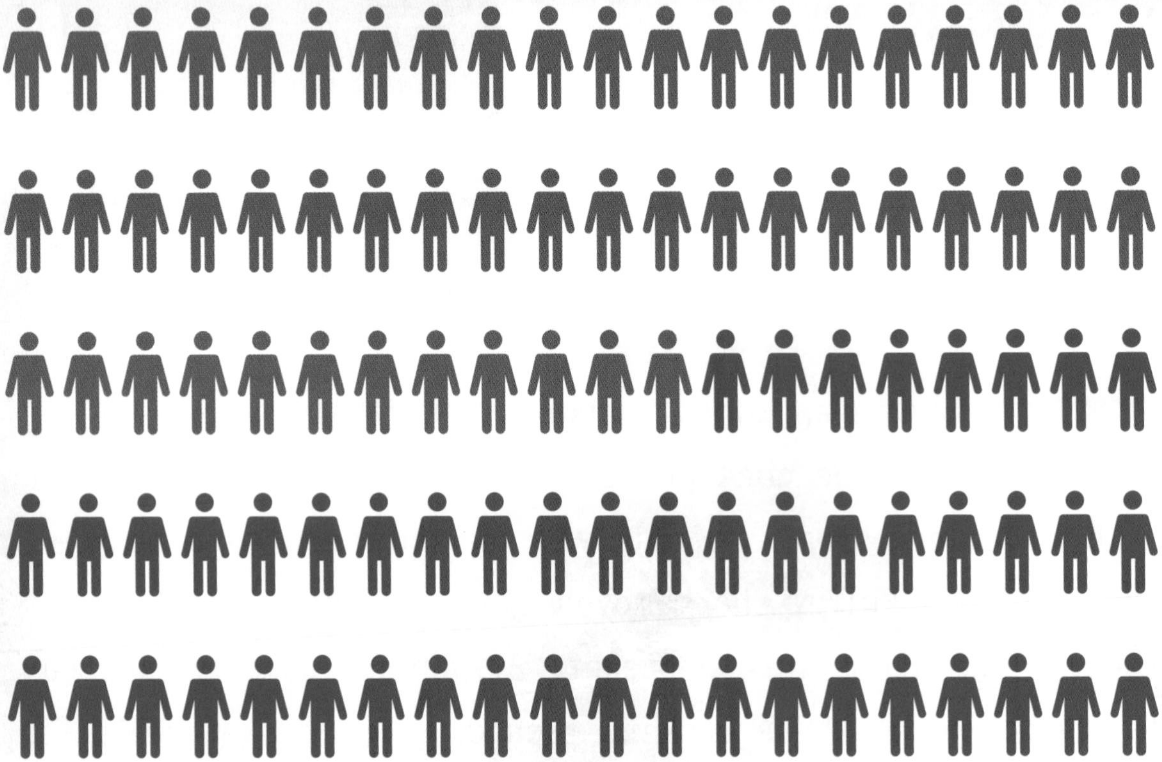

Forty-eight of your neighbors earn less than $2.50 a day.[22] Not only do they have a low income, but the income they do have is sporadic. They may sell a goat or a cow and have a large sum of money one day. However, they have no access to a banking system, so saving is difficult. The lack of a safe place to hold savings can be a major hardship for them.

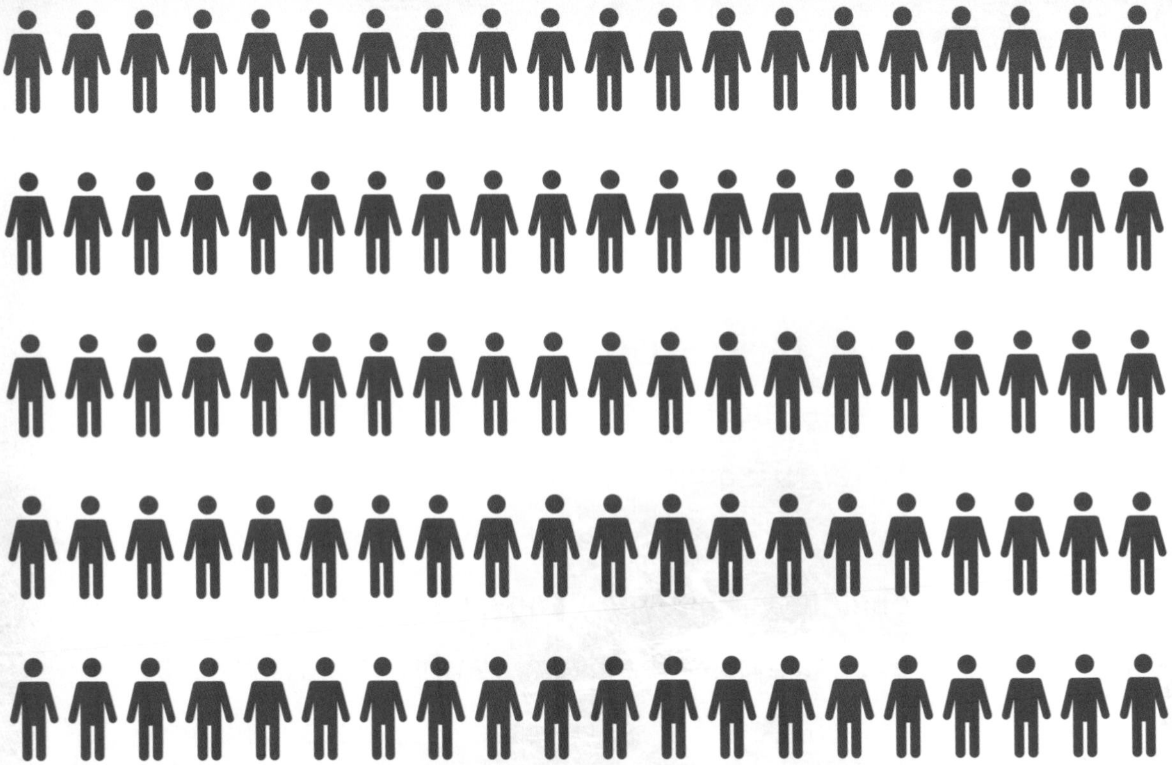

Eighty villagers—by far the majority—
earn less than $10 each day.[23, 24]
Let's visit one of these neighbors
from Bangladesh.

This young Bangla father is trying to provide for his wife and two sons, who live several hours away, by operating a rickshaw in the capital of Dhaka.

After paying the rent on this rickshaw, he is able to earn about $5.70 each day by starting early in the morning and pedaling hard for 14 hours. At night, he sleeps in a room with around forty other men who are doing the same thing. He has been doing this for three years now, and every few weeks he goes home to see his family and take them the money he has saved. His goal is to purchase his own rickshaw and move back home. A new rickshaw costs $115 US, and at the rate he is saving, he should reach his goal in two more years.

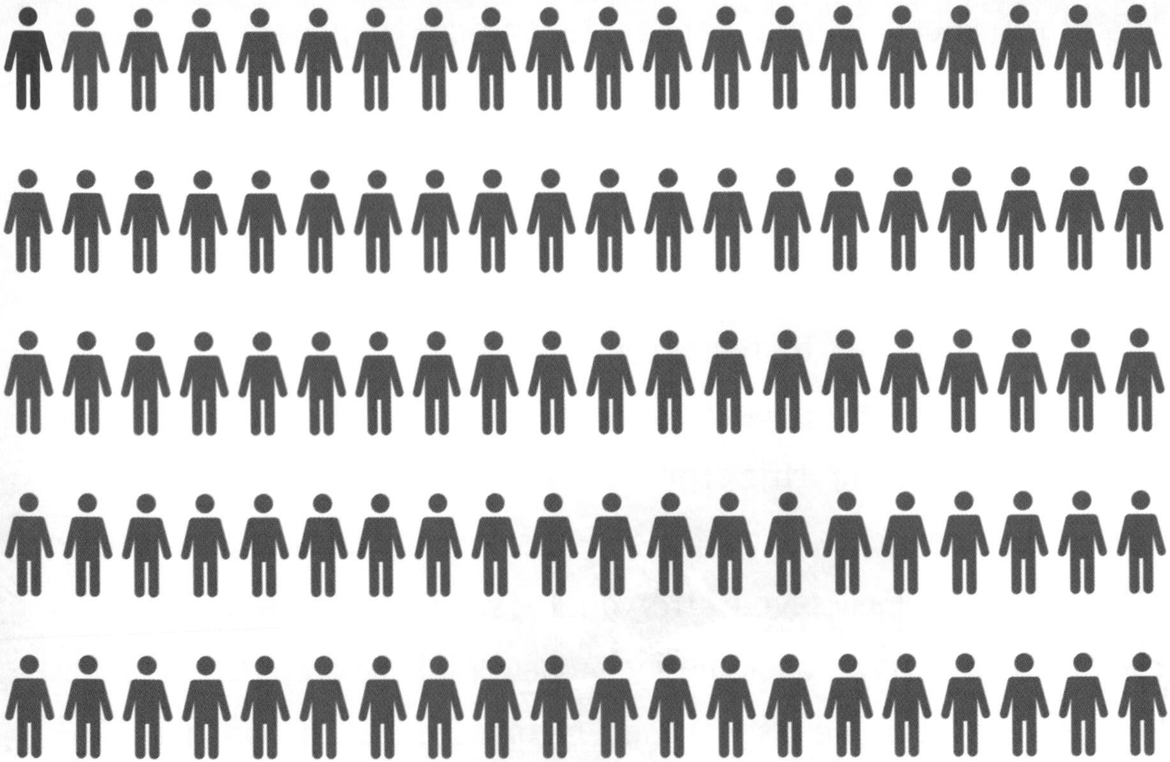

There is only 1 man in your village
who earns more than $34,000 a year.[25]

PERSPECTIVE MATTERS

Living in America can distort our view of reality. But now that we have seen life from a global perspective, when we read Jesus' warnings to the wealthy, we know who He is talking to.

You may live in the United States and feel you are barely earning enough. But what if you lived in a global village? How might living in this village affect your life? Instead of comparing yourself with wealthier people, how would it feel to interact daily with people who have much less than you do?

We tend to isolate ourselves from poverty even within our own country. We are most comfortable associating with people of similar backgrounds and comparable incomes. In a global village, you would be interacting constantly with people who have real needs like food and shelter.

Living in a village like this would affect your point of reference. The constant presence of poverty might change what you regard as normal. Let's look at some ways this greater awareness might affect your choices.

If the United States were a village of 100, you would need to earn $343,000 each year to be the wealthiest man in your village!

RESOURCES

God has placed certain resources into our care, including time, natural abilities, and money. Imagine that all of these are in the green tank labeled RESOURCES. These resources are flowing somewhere, but where?

RESOURCES

NEED

Some resources go to housing—all of us need to live somewhere. Some resources go for food, and of course God intends that we eat. Some resources go for transportation, and some are used for hobbies or other recreation.

 Finally, in many of our lives, the leftover resources go to the spiritual and physical needs of humanity around us.

RESOURCES

NEED

Now imagine a valve on each of the pipes that carry resources to where they are used. God has given us the power to choose the setting on each of these valves. We decide how much we spend on housing and living expenses. We decide how much we spend on transportation or hobbies.
  Sometimes we use so many resources for all these activities that very little is left over for the spiritual and physical needs of others.

RESOURCES

NEED

However, the valves are in our hands. We can share more by consuming less, and I suspect being surrounded by global reality might affect how much we tighten these valves. We might find ourselves using fewer resources on ourselves and sharing more with those in need.

  If you were the wealthiest individual in this village of 100, word would get around fast. People would show up at your house looking for help. In fact, I suspect that within a few days you might open your front door to leave for work and find that your front lawn . . .

. . . looks something like this!

You would begin to understand that you cannot give away enough to supply your village with food and clothing. Even if you tried, you would be out of supplies yourself before long.

Beyond offering handouts, you would need to teach your neighbors a sustainable, Biblical way of life.

WHAT SHOULD WE DO?

We don't really live in a village of 100. However, God knows every person, every need, and every problem in the world. From His perspective, we do live in a global village. How would God have us respond? **Share prayerfully, carefully, and quietly.** All of us need to give. Just as a pond without an outlet will become stagnant, so earning without regular giving will hinder our spiritual growth. As we give, however, we need to be prayerful and discerning so that we don't end up harming the ones we attempt to help.

We also need to give quietly. It is always tempting to make others aware of our good deeds, but we must choose to share without recognition.

Begin at home. When Jesus instructed his disciples to take the message of salvation to the world, He told them to start at home. They were not forbidden to go elsewhere, but they needed to begin where they were. It is easy to neglect mundane tasks at home while chasing the excitement that comes with serving away from home.

Of course, like the lawyer who came to Jesus, we can abuse this principle to narrowly define who our neighbor is. We can choose to live in a nice, secure country setting, ready to help any neighbor who is in need, while knowing that the chance of our neighbors asking for help is extremely small. Let's look for opportunities to begin serving at home.

Remember that we are all of one blood. Although we are called to assist first at home, we need to remember that all humans are part of one family. Even though part of this family lives on the other side of the globe, we still bear responsibility to them. Sometimes, since we don't live in a global village and we

RESPONSIBILITY

What Should I Be Doing?

VS.

OPPORTUNITY

What Could I Be Doing?

rarely see extreme poverty, we forget it exists.

`Look for opportunity.` We can waste time wondering just how many of the world's problems we are responsible to help with. This is exactly the mindset the priest and Levite had in Jesus' story of the Good Samaritan. The priest and the Levite did not believe they were responsible in that situation, so they did not help. But the Samaritan wasn't just trying to figure out the limits of his responsibility; he was looking for opportunities to help! He chose to be a neighbor to the man in need because he saw an opportunity.

`Remember that to whom much is given, much shall be required.` We live in an extremely unusual time. Never before has such a great disparity in wealth existed in our world. Due to global communication and transportation, we are much more aware of needs and can help

a

WORLD
OF OPPORTUNITY

in more ways than ever before. Use the opportunities God has placed before you. Reach out to the struggling in your own congregation, your community, and beyond. Perhaps there has never been a time when Paul's words to the church at Corinth are so applicable. Paul encouraged the Corinthians to share with poor believers living in another country . . . "that now at this time your abundance may be a supply for their want, that their abundance may also be a supply for your want: that there may be equality."[a] May the Lord bless you, "now at this time," as you wisely share what God has placed in your care.

---

[a] 2 Corinthians 8:14

SOURCES

Note: For various reasons, getting exact numbers for population demographics is extremely difficult. Some countries and organizations try to inflate or reduce certain statistics, but I have tried to find as accurate numbers as possible for each statistic. In some cases, this meant averaging statistics from various sources. The numbers in this book are approximate, intended to give an overall picture of our world, and they are always changing. —Gary Miller

DEMOGRAPHICS

[1] "Area and Population of Countries," Information Please Database, 2011, <http://www.infoplease.com/ipa/A0004379.html>, accessed on June 13, 2014.

[2] "World Demographics Profile 2013," Index Mundi, February 21, 2013, <http://www.indexmundi.com/world/demographics_profile.html>, accessed on June 14, 2014.

[3] Matt Rosenberg, "If the World Were a Village," About.com Geography, <http://geography.about.com/od/obtainpopulationdata/a/worldvillage.htm>, accessed on June 13, 2014.

[4] Donella H. Meadows, "State of the Village Report," <http://www.odt.org/Pictures/popvillage.pdf>, accessed on June 13, 2014.

[5] Vaughn Aubuchon, "World Population Growth History," May 29, 2014, <http://www.vaughns-1-pagers.com/history/world-population-growth.htm>, accessed on June 13, 2014.

[6] "World Population by Age and Sex," United States Census Bureau, <http://www.census.gov/population/international/data/idb/worldpop.php>, accessed June 13, 2014.

[7] "Table: Religious Composition by Country, in Numbers," Pew Research Religion & Public Life Project, Pew Research Center, December 18, 2012, <http://www.pewforum.org/2012/12/18/table-religious-composition-by-country-in-numbers>, accessed on June 13, 2014.

[8] The World Factbook, US Central Intelligence Agency, <https://www.cia.gov/library/publications/the-world-factbook/geos/xx.html>, accessed on June 14, 2014.

CHRISTIAN DENOMINATIONS

[9] "Global Christianity – A Report on the Size and Distribution of the World's Christian Population," Pew Research Religion & Public Life Project, Pew Research Center, December 19, 2011, <http://www.pewforum.org/Christian/Global-Christianity-exec.aspx>, accessed on June 14, 2014.

[10] "Protestant Religion," <http://www.religious-beliefs.com/protestant-religion.htm>, accessed on June 14, 2014.

[11] Online summary of research results, Young Center for Anabaptist and Pietist Studies, <http://www.etown.edu/centers/young-center/concise-encyclopedia.aspx>, accessed on June 14, 2014.

[12] "Christian Traditions," Pew Research Religion & Public Life

Project, Pew Research Center, December 19, 2011, <http://www.pewforum.org/2011/12/19/global-christianity-traditions>, accessed on June 14, 2014.

LIFESTYLE AND POVERTY

[13] Anup Shah, "Poverty Facts and Stats," Global Issues, January 7, 2013, <http://www.globalissues.org/article/26/poverty-facts-and-stats>, accessed on June 12, 2014.

[14] "Six in 10 people worldwide lack access to flush toilets or other adequate sanitation," ACS News Service Weekly PressPac, American Chemical Society, March 20, 2013, <http://www.acs.org/content/acs/en/pressroom/presspacs/2013/acs-presspac-march-20-2013/six-in-10-people-worldwide-lack-access-to-flush-toilets-or-other-adequate-sanitation.html>, accessed on June 12, 2014.

[15] "Millions Lack Safe Water," Water.org, <http://water.org/water-crisis/water-facts/water>, accessed on June 12, 2014.

[16] "World Poverty Statistics," July 23, 2012, <http://www.statisticbrain.com/world-poverty-statistics>, accessed on June 12, 2014.

[17] Press Release, "Mobile Phone Access Reaches Three Quarters of Planet's Population," The World Bank, July 17, 2012, <http://www.worldbank.org/en/news/press-release/2012/07/17/mobile-phone-access-reaches-three-quarters-planets-population>, accessed on June 13, 2014.

[18] "World Development Indicators: Traffic and congestion," The World Bank, <http://wdi.worldbank.org/table/3.13>, accessed on June 13, 2014.

[19] "What percentage of the world's population own a car?" <http://wiki.answers.com/Q/What_percentage_of_the_world's_population_own_a_car>, accessed on June 14, 2014.

[20] "Poverty Overview," The World Bank, April 7, 2014, <http://www.worldbank.org/en/topic/poverty/overview>, accessed on June 12, 2014.

[21] Glenn Phelps and Steve Crabtree, "More Than One in Five Worldwide Living in Extreme Poverty," Gallup, December 23, 2013, <http://www.gallup.com/poll/166565/one-five-worldwide-living-extreme-poverty.aspx>, accessed on June 13, 2014.

[22] Shah, <http://www.globalissues.org/article/26/poverty-facts-and-stats>, accessed on June 13, 2014.

[23] <http://www.statisticbrain.com/world-poverty-statistics>, accessed on June 12, 2014.

[24] Shah, <http://www.globalissues.org/article/26/poverty-facts-and-stats>, accessed on June 13, 2014.

[25] "Global Rich List," Poke, <http://www.globalrichlist.com>, accessed on June 12, 2014.

OTHER RESOURCES BY THE AUTHOR

Gary Miller was raised in an Anabaptist community in California and today lives with his wife Patty and family in the Pacific Northwest. Gary's enthusiasm for Kingdom building has prompted him to produce the resources listed on this page, all published by TGS International.

KINGDOM-FOCUSED LIVING SERIES

Kingdom-Focused Finances for the Family | This first book is serious about getting us to become stewards instead of owners. *240 pages*

Charting a Course in Your Youth | A serious call to youth to examine their faith, focus, and finances. *211 pages*

Going Till You're Gone | A plea for older men and women to demonstrate a Kingdom-focused vision all the way to the finish line. *281 pages*

The Other Side of the Wall | Encourages all Christians to reflect God's heart in giving, whether by helping in their local community or by seeking to alleviate poverty abroad. *250 pages*

OTHER BOOKS/MANUALS

Budgeting Made Simple | A budgeting workbook in a ring binder; complements *Kingdom-Focused Finances for the Family.*

What Happened to Our Money? | An introductory financial guide for young couples. *4.25" x 7" | 86 pages*

Small Business Handbook | A microfinance manual used in developing countries. Includes devotionals and practical business teaching. Ideal for missions and churches. *8.5" x 11" | spiral bound | 136 pages*

Following Jesus in Everyday Life | A second microfinance manual that sets the stage for group discussions on how to follow Jesus daily in personal and business matters. *8.5" x 11" | spiral bound | 93 pages*

AUDIO AND POWER POINT SEMINARS

Kingdom-Focused Finances Seminar—3 audio CDs
This three-session seminar challenges you to examine your heart by looking at your treasure.

Kingdom-Focused Finances Seminar Audio PowerPoint—3 CDs
On your computer, you can now view the slides Gary uses in his seminars while you listen to the presentation. A good tool for group study or individual use.

AUDIO BOOKS, NARRATED BY THE AUTHOR

Kingdom-Focused Finances for the Family, Charting a Course in Your Youth, Going Till You're Gone, and **The Other Side of the Wall.**